MW00564476

Suzuki

CELLO SCHOOL

Volume 1
Cello Part
International Edition

AMPV: 1.01

Copyright © 2018, 2014, 2007, 1978 International Suzuki Association
Sole publisher for the entire world except Japan:
Summy-Birchard, Inc.
Exclusive print rights administered by Alfred Music
All rights reserved. Printed in USA.

Available in the following formats: Book (0479S), Book & CD Kit (40697), CD (0940)

Book	Book & CD Kit
ISBN-10: 0-87487-479-3	ISBN-10: 0-7390-9709-1
ISBN-13: 978-0-87487-479-2	ISBN-13: 978-0-7390-9709-0

INTRODUCTION

FOR THE STUDENT: This volume is part of the worldwide Suzuki Method of teaching. The companion recording should be used along with this publication. A piano accompaniment book is also available for this material.

FOR THE TEACHER: In order to be an effective Suzuki teacher, ongoing education is encouraged. Each regional Suzuki association provides teacher development for its membership via conferences, institutes, short-term and long-term programs. In order to remain current, you are encouraged to become a member of your regional Suzuki association, and, if not already included, the International Suzuki Association.

FOR THE PARENT: Credentials are essential for any Suzuki teacher you choose. We recommend you ask your teacher for his or her credentials, especially those related to training in the Suzuki Method. The Suzuki Method experience should foster a positive relationship among the teacher, parent and child. Choosing the right teacher is of utmost importance.

In order to obtain more information about the Suzuki Association in your region, please contact:

International Suzuki Association
www.internationalsuzuki.org

CONTENTS

学習と指導の目標

指導上の４つの要点

1．子どもに、できるだけ毎日レコードを聞かせることによって音楽的感覚を向上させる。それは同時によりはやい進歩をうながす。

2．トナリゼイション、つまり美しい音の指導を、教室や家庭においてかならず行なわれなければならない。

3．不断の注意によって、正しい音程、正しい姿勢、正しい弓の持ち方ができるように。

4．親も先生も、子どもが家庭でたのしくしっかり練習するように努力する。

以上の４つのポイントを徹底して行なうことによって、どの子どもも音楽的才能がよく育つことを、私は30年にわたる教育の経験からはっきりと確信するようになりました。

音楽の才能は生まれつきのものではなく、育てられるものなのです。それはちょうど、日本の子どもがだれでも日本語を話し、世界中の子どもが、みなそれぞれの母国語をじょうずに話しているのと同じように、音楽もその育て方にしたがって、どの子どもにも育てられる能力であり、聞けばよく育ちます。

どうぞ子どものしあわせのために、この４つのポイントが、家庭や教室において十分成功するように指導を行なってください。

Four Essential Points for Teachers and Parents

1. Children should listen to the reference recordings every day at home to develop musical sensitivity. Rapid progress depends on this listening.
2. Tonalization, or the production of a beautiful tone, should be stressed in the lesson and at home.
3. Constant attention should be given to accurate intonation, correct posture, and the proper bow hold.
4. Parents and teachers should strive to motivate children so they will enjoy practicing correctly at home.

Through the experience I have gained in teaching young children for over thirty years, I am thoroughly convinced that musical ability can be fully cultivated in all children if the above four points are faithfully observed.

Musical ability is not an inborn talent but an ability that can be developed. All children who are properly trained can develop musical ability just as all children develop the ability to speak their mother tongue. For the happiness of children, I hope these four essential points will be carefully observed and put to continual use in the home and in the studio.

Shinichi Suzuki

The D-string Posture is fundamental and should be completely mastered.

Exercises for Proper D-String Posture

Use a short bow stroke.

Exercises for Changing Strings

Exercises for Quick Placement of Fingers

Place fingers 1,2,3,4 quickly and accurately during the rests.

When playing the 4th finger, keep all four fingers down on the string.

The First Position

The purpose of the following exercises is to play the notes accurately.
Press the string with the tip of finger.

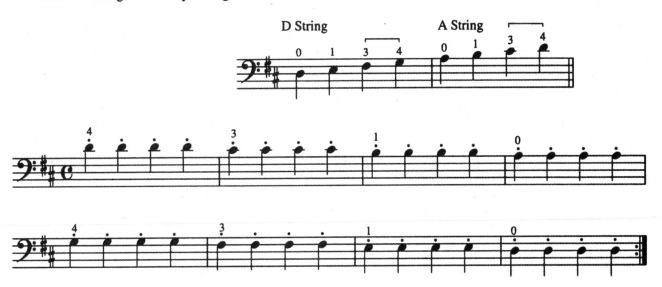

a) Play the 4th finger, keeping the 1st, 2nd and 3rd fingers down on the string.
   While playing the 4th finger, think and prepare for the next position of your finger.
   Repeat on the A string.
b) For half a year, at least, continue the practice of stopping the bow on the string after each note to get a **clear sound.**

D Major Scale

While playing the upper half of the scale, the 1st and the 3rd fingers should remain on the string.
When you place the 3rd finger, place the 2nd down with it.

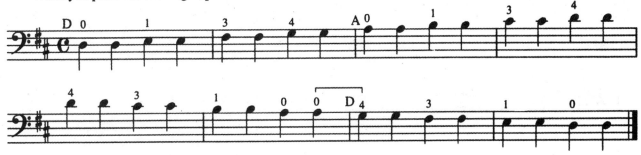

Important Instructions for Practice:
The fingering $\overline{0\ 4}$ requires very careful practice. Stop the bow after you play open A, and be sure to place
the first, second, third, and fourth fingers in the proper position on the D string before you continue to play.

1 Twinkle, Twinkle, Little Star Variations

To play ♪♫ stop the bow without pressure after each note.

Bow ♫♫ smoothly.

S. Suzuki

2 French Folk Song

To develop the practice of tonalization

Folk Song

3 Lightly Row

Folk Song

Keep the 3rd finger down.

1

11

4 Song of the Wind

Folk Song

Keep the 1st finger down.

5 Go Tell Aunt Rhody

Folk Song

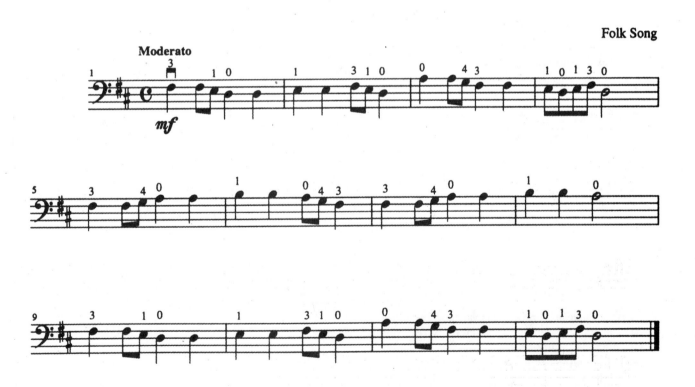

6 O Come, Little Children

Folk Song

Tonalization

This should be taught at each lesson.
Pluck the open string and listen to the sound of the vibrating string.

Play tones with the same resonance with the bow.

Questions teachers and parents must ask every day :
Are the pupils listening to the reference record at home every day ?
Has the tone improved ?
Is the intonation correct ?
Has the proper playing posture been acquired ?
Is the bow being held correctly ?

7 May Song

Folk Song

8 Allegro

S. Suzuki

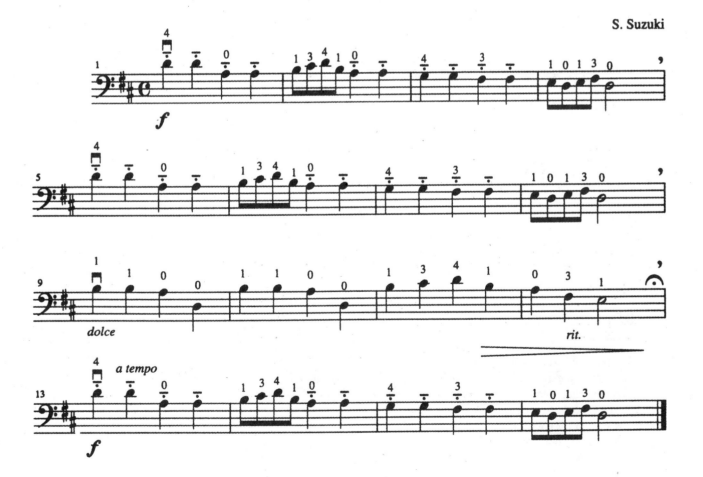

9 Perpetual Motion in D Major

Play this piece at the middle of the bow using a very short stroke.
Stop the bow after each note.
Play slowly at first and then gradually speed up the tempo.

S. Suzuki

Variation

After A, play B,

Procedure for practice:

etc.

Transpose all previous pieces to the key of G Major in preparation for "Long, Long Ago."

Tonalization

This should be taught at each lesson. Pupils should
always strive for a more beautiful and resonant tone.

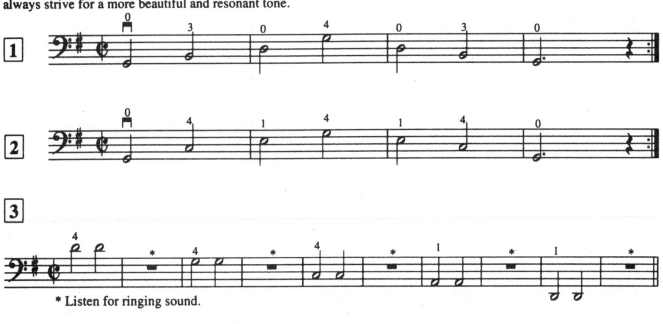

* Listen for ringing sound.

G Major Scale

Perpetual Motion in G Major

S. Suzuki

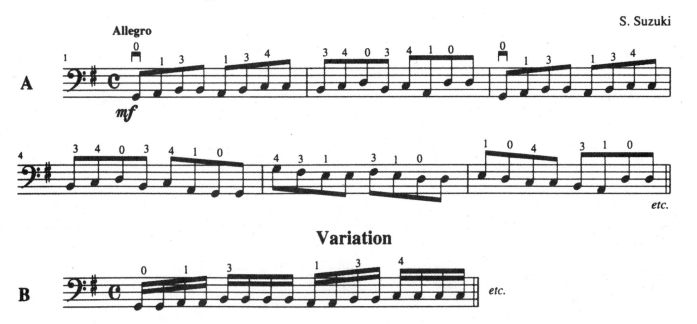

Variation

10 Long, Long Ago

T. H. Bayly

11 Allegretto

S. Suzuki

12 Andantino

S. Suzuki

Second-Finger Training
(Preparatory Exercise for "Rigadoon")

* Lift third & fourth fingers together

13 Rigadoon

H. Purcell

* See P. 17, second finger training, for preparatory exercise using 2nd finger.

Tonalization
This should be taught at each lesson.

C Major Scale
(Two Octaves)

14 Etude

Stop the bow after each note.

S. Suzuki

Variation

15 The Happy Farmer

Allegro giocoso

R. Schumann

16 Minuet in C

Grazioso

J. S. Bach

(2nd time) poco rit.

17 Minuet No. 2

J. S. Bach

Before playing this piece see diagrams and pictures on pages 22 & 23.

G# Exercise

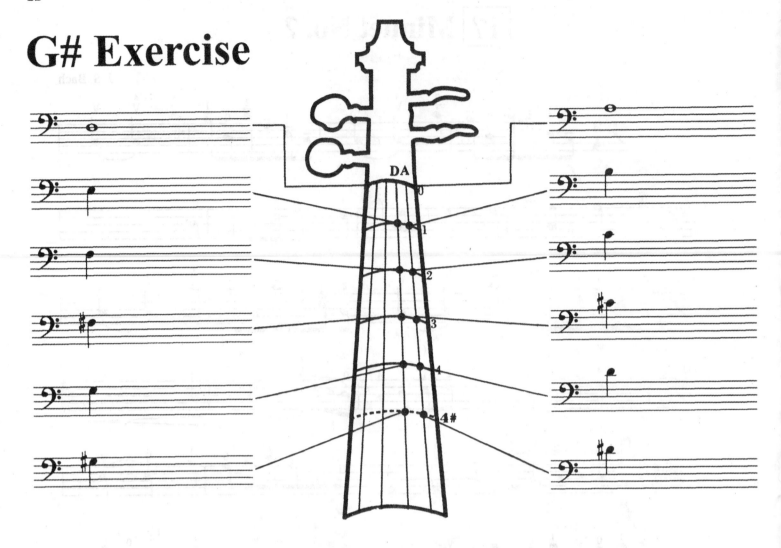

Closed First Position

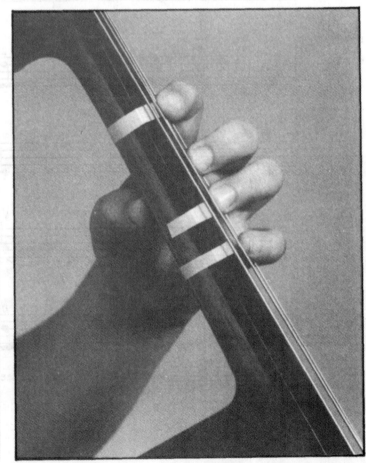

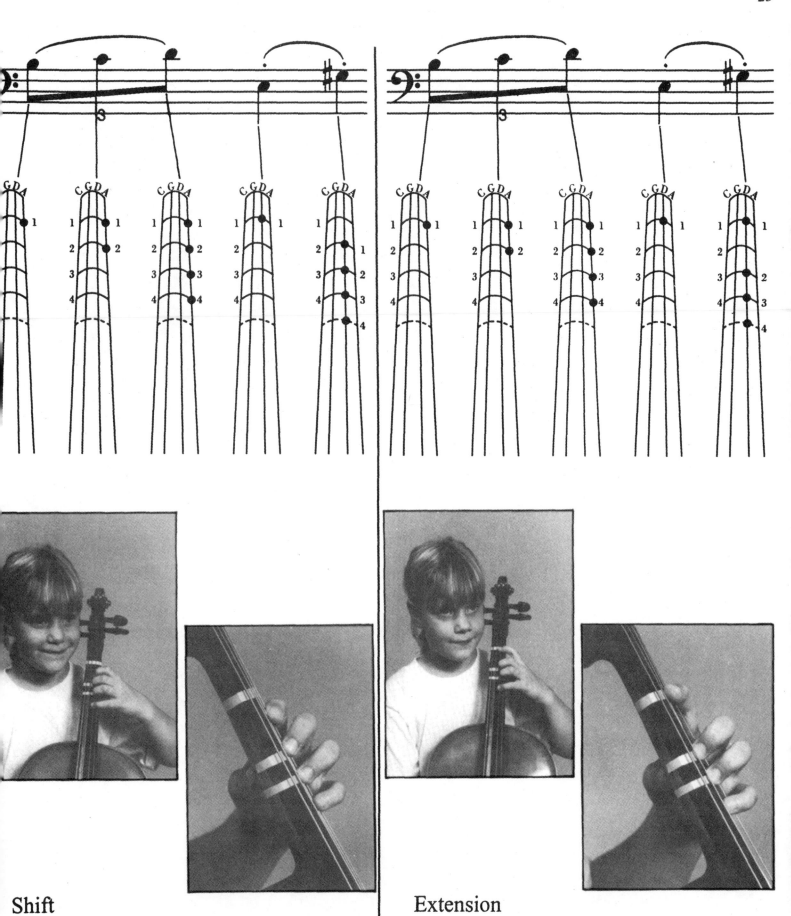

Shift

Explanation

[Mo]ve all fingers and thumb one-half step higher. (Keep [thu]mb under 2).

Extension

Explanation

Move 2, 3, 4 and thumb one-half step higher. (Keep thumb under 2). Bring elbow forward for extension.